MW00718425

The Pursuit of Purpose, Passion & Performance

Baylor Barbee

Idea of Excellence: *The Pursuit of Purpose, Passion & Performance*

Copyright © 2014 by Baylor Barbee

Cover Design: Jeremy Biggers

Editing: Marchella Simon

Creative Consultation: Jasmin Brand

ISBN: 978-0-692-20623-2

To my parents, Wil and Renee Barbee

Thank you for teaching me to give my all to whatever I do, never quit on a dream, and above all, always have Faith.

You are the true definition of Excellence.

Why I Wrote this Book

I would love to tell you that I set out on a journey to write about excellence, but that'd be a lie. The truth is, when I embarked on the journey to write this book, the focus was on success. Success is the thing we all crave, isn't it? We all want successful relationships, businesses, friendships, and lives.

It seemed like the perfect topic. As I continued to research success, I noticed there was a select group of people, though they didn't seem to have any external advantages in life, that rose to the ranks of legendary, far exceeding the accomplishments of those "successful" people.

These people didn't all amass great wealth, but each of them possessed a quality that not all successful people had. They lived a life of fulfillment. What they stood for outlived them. What they believed in still inspires people today. That's much more than success.

That journey led me to figure out what it was that made these men and women stand apart from successful people as legends and icons.

I first looked at my own life and the successes I've had. Where did they come from? I thought back to how my parents raised me and my brother and sister. My parents were highly decorated collegiate athletes. As a result, we were involved in sports our entire lives. My siblings and I won state championships in various sports and all received athletic scholarships. But it was more than just "success."

I asked myself, WHY did we continually win as children growing up? Was it because we were the most athletically talented people on the field or court? Chances are, there may have been a more physically gifted individual. Why did we excel in school? Were we the smartest? We may have been, but perhaps there was someone out there who was smarter.

I realized it wasn't "success" that my parents tried to instill in us. *We didn't win because we were the best.*

We were the best because we outworked everyone, in everything.

It was an attitude that my parents instilled in us that has shaped who we are as people today. It's an attitude of excellence. Focusing on a task, working relentlessly to achieve that feat, picking a greater task, and repeating. Getting to the soccer field two hours before the other kids and staying an hour extra everyday wasn't just about winning; it was about excellence. Those holidays spent in the gym instead of lying on the couch playing video games weren't about W's; it was about excellence. The fact that we weren't allowed to bring home less than a 94 on a report card because it was "too close to a B" wasn't about the grade; it was about holding ourselves to a higher standard and pursuing our best.

This attitude, this idea of excellence, I realized, is what separated mere successful people from legends.

Excellence is something many have heard of, but few really understand. In my research, I found a whole lot of information about success, very little about excellence.

This book was written for two purposes. First, I want to help you define excellence by painting a picture of what it truly is. Second, I want to give you the tools necessary to achieve excellence in your life by highlighting the five qualities that all men and women of excellence possess.

Yes, I wish you abundant success in your life. But more than success, I want you to live a life of fulfillment. At the end of your days, I want your life to count for something more than just a trophy on the wall or a large number in your bank account. It is my hope that your life is filled with catching dreams and realizing potentials.

Welcome to the Idea of Excellence.

Table of Contents

Chapter 1 – Why Choose Excellence

There are three types of people in the world. There are those who see the glass half full, those who see the glass half empty, and a third class of people. Excellence is the group of people who don't concern themselves with whether the glass is half full or half empty, but rather focus on how to fill the glass.

Excellence is continually striving for something greater than you. It's not only squeezing all of the juice out of the lemon, it's then figuring out how to use the lemon peel to aid in creating better lemonade. It's maximizing your potential.

I've spent the last few years obsessively pursuing this idea of excellence. I've studied countless businessmen, coaches, athletes, philosophers, visionaries, monks and more to find out what truly defines excellence. Excellence, ironically, is a term often used, but rarely defined.

How do you define excellence?

What are the qualities of excellence? What separates the legendary people of the ages, the .001% from the other 99.999% of people? After all, we're all made of essentially the same genetic makeup. Sure, some have skills that others don't have and are born with, yet history shows us that is not an indicator of excellence.

Many "privileged" people fall into mediocrity while many who are deemed under-privileged, rise to great heights. Why is this?

This is the question that always puzzled me. If excellence isn't based on circumstance or situation, what is it that truly sets us apart? Is it something we are all capable of, or is excellence purely meant for a select few?

After studying the lives, philosophies, and work of many of the greatest people in history, I've come to realize that the ability to truly excel is available to us all.

However, it's if and only if, we know how to define and achieve excellence in our lives.

After all, how can you ever reach a destination if you don't know where it is or what you're looking for? Too many go in search of this grand idea of greatness, success, or excellence, without the slightest clue for what they're actually looking.

We all want to be successful, right? Have you ever actually asked yourself what success means to you? It's easy to say "I want to make more money," or "I want to get a better job," but is that really success? By success, I mean, will that really fulfill you? If you make one more dollar than you do now, would that not be a success based on what you said? If you got a job with a better title on a business card, did anything really change?

The illusion of success can be a rat race that never ends. Success really is your ability to be better than those around you. That doesn't mean you're living to the best of your ability though. *Perhaps you're "winning" in the loser's bracket.*

So what do we do to avoid that travesty? Focus on excellence. If success is being better than others, then excellence is the continual mastery of self.

Like many of us, I love cheering for my country during the Olympics. I particularly love watching the sprint events, man versus man, for the title of the fastest human in the world. The peak of athletic success, right? It never fails in every Olympics, a runner has a big lead, looks over his shoulder to see where his competition is, and what happens? You guessed it, he gets passed on the other side.

Was he the fastest man on the track? Most likely he was. But in the end, the results showed otherwise. What was his problem? The runner, like many of us in life, focused on success. He gauged his abilities by how well he compared to others on the track. When he thought he gave enough to be the best, he turned to see how others' best effort measured up to his. What did the winner do? He focused on running his best race. He focused on excellence.

Excellence understands that great results happen to those who focus solely on doing their best with no regard to how well everyone else may seem to be doing.

Excellence understands that this marathon of life is a long race and the appearance of others' successes is no guarantee that things will always be that way. Case in point, looking at long distance events in the Summer Olympics, often a participant will be further ahead than the rest of the contestants; a seemingly easy win... Success right?

But, what's happening inside? Too often that pacesetter runs out of gas and quickly gets caught and passed at the end by those who ran their race...excellence.

When you focus on getting the best out of yourself, you won't ever be completely disappointed with the results because you know that you earned the best possible outcome for your ability.

In the long run, excellence always beats success. There are always roadblocks or hurdles on the path to success. External factors affect our ability to succeed. Excellence, however, is internal. You have full control over your ability to give your best effort to each and every day, and that should excite you.

At the end of the day, a life of fulfillment comes from excellence, not success. Success is fleeting, excellence is everlasting. I'm by no means saying don't strive to be successful. I am saying that focusing on excellence will allow you to reach the height of success in all areas of your life. More importantly, you'll reach those pinnacles in a much more fulfilled, content manner.

From Farms to Hall of Fame

As a young boy, he moved to a farm in a small Indiana town as one of six siblings. He went on to become a great basketball player for his high school and collegiate teams. He earned money playing professional basketball and coaching high school basketball at the same time until, like most young men his age, World War 2 came along and he loaned his services to the United States Navy. This may seem like a neat little story of a small town boy who was athletic and served his country well. That in itself would be considered a success. However, this man's journey only just began.

John Wooden, undoubtedly the greatest coach in the history of college basketball, was the epitome of excellence. As the head coach of the UCLA Bruins, he won 10 National championships in 12 years, including 7 championships in a row. He won every conceivable award known to the coaching industry to the point where the greatest awards are named in his honor.

How did a farm boy become the all-time winningest coach who set records that may never be touched?

He focused on Excellence.

Unlike many other coaches who focused solely on what it took to win, John Wooden focused on what it took to develop better young men, on and off the court. He believed in all-around excellence. He didn't simply believe in teaching the X's and O's necessary to win basketball games, but the X's and O's that create a proper foundation for his student athletes to succeed in the field of life. By creating habits in these young men, winning games became a bi-product of who they were   as   young   men.

His philosophy, though it sounds counterculture to what we may believe, was validated by his results; success as we call it. His philosophy was this, "it's not whether you won or lost, it's if you played your best game." He said you can outscore a team and not play your best, that's not a win in life. You can get outscored by a team and have played your best, that's not a loss. By ingraining the idea of giving your best effort and not focusing on the outcome of the game, you'll get the result you're looking for more times than not.

In his case, 664 times it worked, only 162 times it did not. That means over 8 out of every 10 games, he won by focusing on excellence. No matter what you're trying to achieve in life, would you not take those odds? What if you knew you'd close 8 out of every 10 deals you tried to reach? You'd probably be sitting pretty well right now, would you not? Wooden did it by focusing on excellence and sticking to those values. He probably could have won a couple of games that he lost due to sticking to his strict moral code of conduct that had him benching star players who didn't do what was required of the remainder of the team, but perhaps he would have then lost a lot more games too. Excellence always wins in the end.

From Unpaid Sketches to Immortality

Born the son of a minister, he was a quiet introspective boy. Though he always had a passion for sketches and the arts, he tried to follow in the footsteps of his family and become a minister. After apprenticeships, he failed numerous exams to become a minister, thus defaulting to jobs such as supply teachers and ultimately a missionary for a mining city. He developed a mental illness and excessively smoked and drank hard liquor. However, his love for drawing and painting never died, though he did at the young age of 37 from an alleged self-inflicted wound.

This is a book about excellence, right? What's the lesson here? Tragic story with an even more tragic ending, right? If you were to base his success on what he accomplished and was credited for while living, then yes, this wouldn't be much of a story. However, if you look at the definition of excellence in the arts, very few would argue that Vincent Van Gogh was one the all-time greats as his paintings now sell for millions of dollars.

While alive, it's believed that Van Gogh only sold one painting, but Van Gogh wasn't after the money or worldly success being a famous painter could bring. Vincent painted because of how it made him feel. He painted because it brought his thoughts and emotions to life, despite battling severe anxiety and depression. He painted and drew to improve. To this day, his hundreds of sketches and paintings are revered in the most famous museums and art houses in the world. That's true excellence.

A Harry Fortune

Depressed from the loss of her mother, freshly out of a divorce from a short marriage, alone with an infant child and living on welfare, the odds were stacked against Joanne. She lived in a government subsidized, unheated house, covered in rats, which was no place for a small infant. She fought to stay in coffee shops for long periods of time so that her daughter could sleep in a warm location while she wrote a 700 page novel by hand; and typed on an old school manual typewriter. Day after day, Joanne continued to write this fantasy story about a small boy and his special school while barely being able to survive. After finishing her fantasy story, the novel was promptly rejected by dozens of publishing houses in the UK.

Most in her situation, desperate and poor, would have given up and found another way to "be successful," or even worse, "get by." Joanne, like those few who achieve true excellence, was focused on getting her story heard. She was driven to find someone to give her story a chance.

She never looked at the odds or the possibility of failing. She saw the potential and what it could be if she stayed on course. Now, with over 400 million books sold, the first billionaire author of all time, J. K. Rowling's fantasy story about a young boy is world renowned and you know it by another name, Harry Potter.

It's Inside You

Based on their upbringing and story, none of the aforementioned models of excellence seemingly had any significant advantages over any other coach, painter, or author. What they did possess was an unrelenting drive to continually improve upon their passion.

That same drive is available to you right now. No one can give it to you and no can take it away.

Regardless of your circumstance or situation, you have the ability to bridge the gap between where you are and what you're capable of becoming. Here's a secret. You're capable of becoming far greater than you already are.

Are you ready to make that commitment to excellence? Are you ready to pursue and find your purpose, live with passion and exceedingly outperform your current self in all areas of your life whether it be financial, relationships, health, or faith? If so, you're on the path to excellence.

Why choose excellence? You owe it to yourself to get the most out of your own life.

Chapter 2 – Inspiration vs Motivation

I'm privileged and honored to be able to travel and speak across the country and conduct webinars worldwide. I've been fortunate to speak to everyone from kindergarteners, to churches, youth groups, businesses, colleges, teams and more. You name it, I've probably spoken to them. One thing I never do is tell the host of the event how to introduce me.

I've always found it fascinating what accolades the different moderators and hosts find impressive and use to introduce me. I've probably never cared, since in my mind, though blessed to have achieved some nice feats, I am still at the base of the mountain of achievement that I'm trying to climb. Aside from that, I'm not there to toot my own horn, but to spark life into the ability of the audience to catch their dreams. It never fails though; in 99% of introductions, after a list of achievements, degrees and athletic scholarships, comes the dreaded "He's a (insert adjective) …. MOTIVATIONAL SPEAKER. Ughh, I hate that word.

I don't think the hosts mean anything negative by it. In fact, I guess I should view it as an honor to be viewed as motivational. But, as I've grown and studied the legends, I have learned a very valuable lesson. Motivation isn't enough.

It's better to Treat than To Cure

You don't have to be a genius to realize there is more money in treating symptoms for a long period of time than there is in curing the disease of the patient. Why else would drug companies create numerous new drugs every single year to treat various symptoms? Every pharmacy is lined with rows and rows of drugs that "temporarily relieve pain." Back pain, headaches, sore throats, you name it, there is a drug to make it feel better…for 4-6 hours. Many become addicted to the cycles of these temporary pain relievers, which is good for the companies selling them. I challenge you to go to a drug store and count the amount of times you see "temporary pain relief" versus "permanent removal of the symptom." Why is this? There's more money in treating an issue than curing the cause.

Is this a rant on the drug industry? Absolutely not. They do some wonderful things and save a lot of lives as well, but the parallel to motivation is one in the same. Motivation will temporarily make you feel good, but it won't last. Like temporary pain relief, it makes you feel good for a couple of hours and then real life hits. You are faced again with your problems, your bills, your stresses and worries, and the motivation tends to go away. The motivation is replaced with "I'll get to it tomorrow" which we all know means never. Finally, you get caught in the same cycle and need more "motivation."

Perhaps that's why it seems like everybody I meet now, and 90% of people on social sites, are now "Motivational Speakers." Seems like a great industry. People find a few clever sayings that can get people pumped up, package that and sell it as a speech or a course, simple right?

But I truly believe we mislabel what we're really after when we say we need more motivation. It's not that I don't want people leaving my speeches or seminars feeling unstoppable. It's that I want them to actually become unstoppable, for good.

Do you want temporary "motivation" or do you want permanent drive?

Do you want gasoline, which requires numerous fill-ups to keep you moving, or would you prefer to have the unlimited energy of the sun?

That unlimited energy, that permanent drive, is inspiration. *If motivation is the building block of success, then inspiration is the foundation behind excellence.*

With every piece of content I write or words I speak, my aim is to inspire. Therefore, it's not my goal to motivate, but to truly inspire, to light that fire in those who hear me. Believe me, when your passion is set on fire, you'll find a way to attain anything you want to have.

What is it that you are truly passionate about? Before you go any further, answer that question. What is it that you could gladly jump out of bed each day with extreme excitement and spend endless hours pursuing or participating in We each have something that we wouldn't need others to "motivate" us to want to do. Motivation is external. Inspiration is that source within yourself that keeps you fired up. What's your passion? Once you truly discover your passion, you'll no longer worry about the fear of failure or the chance that you might not get to your goal because the burning desire of what you COULD be will keep you moving forward… and you will become it.

Yo ADRIAN, I DID IT!

You'd be hard pressed to find someone who hasn't seen one of the Rocky movies or at least knows who Rocky is. We all loved the never quit attitude of Rocky, portrayed by Sylvester Stallone, as quotes and clips from the movie are often used as motivational pieces. The true inspirational story is not in Rocky's ability to take punishment and win fights against seemingly indestructible opponents, but what Stallone had to do to make Rocky happen.

You might not recognize the accent of Stallone, but that's probably due to the fact that he was born with a paralysis on the lower part of his face, which slurred his speech. Aside from that, he had very little to his name, yet set out to New York City to become an actor. Stallone famously stated that he'd been turned down over 1,500 times by casting directors and agencies. The problem was that there weren't even

1,500 agencies in New York, to which Stallone replied, some turned me down more than once.

At this point, any motivated person would have lost their motivation. Things got so bad for Stallone that he had to sell his beloved dog for $25 just to survive. In his despair, he got an idea. After watching a Muhammad Ali fight, he stayed up all weekend writing a script about a boxer who overcame all the odds, a true people's champ.

He found a producer who was willing to buy the script for $125,000 dollars on the one condition that Sylvester couldn't act in the movie. A desperate person, "motivated" to succeed, would have gladly taken the money, which would be a seeming fortune. Stallone was not motivated, he was inspired. His dream was to be an actor. He walked away.

Before we go any further, *ask yourself this. Is the passion or vision in your life strong enough that you'd turn down good things in order to pursue what you're really after or are you willing to settle for "good enough?"* Inspired people accept nothing less than the most that life can offer.

Weeks went by as he continued to starve. The studio presented him an offer a motivated person couldn't refuse, $325,000. That's a fortune to someone who had spent weeks sleeping in bus terminals. But again, Stallone was inspired to act. Finally, the studio agreed to let him act, but would only pay him $35,000.

Stallone immediately tracked down the dog he sold for $25 dollars and finally was able to buy his dog back…for $15,000! A "motivated" person would say that's insane. To an uninspired person, inspiration does and should seem crazy. It's the crazy people who change the world. *When you're inspired, you're consumed with the vision and purpose, not the appearance of what others deem realistic.*

The Rocky franchise went on to make hundreds of millions of dollars all because Stallone's inspiration would not let him settle for less than his best. Do you have a dream you're willing to stop at nothing to achieve? Find a way to ignite that fire of inspiration into your passion and it will be so.

Remove the "how can I get motivated" from your vocabulary right now and replace it with "how can I become inspired?" That's the million-dollar question. The answer is easier than you might think.

Those looking for motivation rely on outside factors; people, places, material objects, etc. I'm sure you could motivate most people to do just about anything if you set $1,000,000 in cash right in front of them. But how do you get the same results out of people without the need for external stimulus? As a business owner, a manager, a coach or a leader, this is an invaluable skill that will produce far greater results with far greater satisfaction than motivation.

The answer to how to find inspiration in yourself and to inspire it in others is to look inside, not outside. Don't ask yourself, what can get me this result? Ask yourself, how can I add value to the task at hand? How can it be done better? What can I do to enjoy this task? In answering these question, you'll find your inspiration. The small difference in how you frame what you're doing in your mind, makes all the long term difference in the world.

Motivation says: How many more cars do I need to sell get my bonus?

Inspiration says: How can I become an added value to this dealership and to my customers?

Motivation says: How can I get motivated to lose weight?
Inspiration says: Don't I owe it to my family to remain healthy in order be there for them?

Motivation says: I wish someone would invent....
Inspiration says: Why don't I create...

If you look closely, you'll notice all motivation based questions we ask ourselves require someone else adding value to our lives. I hate to be the bearer of bad news, but we live in a "me, me, me" society where the majority of people are looking for what they can get. If you're waiting on someone else to help you get going, you'll be waiting a long time.

Inspiration based questions are a complete reversal. They involve you asking yourself how you can help other people. If you do the opposite of everyone else, you'll always be in demand. Remember, we live in a society of takers, why not give? Furthermore, I've realized if you're only out to conquer a dream or reach a new height for yourself, you'll quit when you get tired or things don't go your way. When you are inspired to achieve, whether it be for your family, friends, or the ideal itself, quitting isn't even a word in your vocabulary.

Small changes make large differences. You can fuel your own vehicle on the road to the best you, or you can hitchhike on the road to wherever the world will take you. (Hint, it will never give you a free ride to where you want to go.) In knowing this, why wouldn't you decide to take the driver's seat in your own life?

My inbox is filled with hundreds of emails from people who aren't happy with their lives and 99% of the people say the same thing; "(insert person or situation) did (insert sad story) to me, and that's why I can't (insert pipe dream)." I ask all of them the same question; why don't you take the steering wheel and jump in the driver's seat of your own life?

Sounds so simple, yet so many are afraid to live life on their own terms instead of the "standard way of life" (whatever that's supposed to mean) that they feel they are supposed to live. Motivation might get your blood pumping and get your vehicle moving a little faster, but you're still on the road to mediocrity and eventually, just like a car that you've pushed too hard, you'll run out of gas.

Inspiration, on the other hand, will have you creating your own path, because you're not bound to the same fuel stops and rest stops that "motivated" people need to refuel. Think about what inspires you. Are you on the road to what that inspiration calls you to do? If not, it's probably time to fuel yourself and take a hard exit off the "safe" path you're on.

Besides, life is more fun off-road anyway!

Chapter 3 – The Standard of Excellence

In early March of 1836, after having fought for nearly two weeks against an army numerous times the size of his own, Colonel William Travis of the Texas Army knew the chance of winning the battle at the Alamo was virtually impossible. The Mexican general, Santa Anna, sent a letter to the colonel demanding the surrender of what was left of the Texas troops, or he promised to kill every one of them.

The Texans were surrounded, with more Mexican reinforcements continually arriving. Colonel Travis gathered all his men together, less than 200 remaining, and read the letter requesting their surrender, to his fellow defenders of the Alamo. After reading the letter, he took his sword and slowly drew a line in the sand and stepped across it. The line was symbolic in stating that any man who stepped across that line was not turning back, they would die for their country. All but one stepped across that line. All those who stepped across the line, died as heroes fighting for their freedom the next morning.

The line in the sand is a perfect metaphor for our own lives and how we continue to evolve and flourish. The important thing to decide, however, is where you draw that line in the sand in your own life.

There are two options. Most people draw a line in the sand far into the future of their lives. The name of that line is usually called goals. Goals are some imaginary finish lines most hope to cross "one day." If you have goals, ponder for a second the language you use when thinking about them. Often we tell ourselves, "one day I want to get a promotion," or "it's my goal to make a million dollars," or "I'm hoping to buy a house."

These goals become ideals or dreams that we "hope" to accomplish. Is hope enough to get us across that line when things get tough? It's hard to stay focused on a future line in the sand ahead of you when you're bogged down with the problems of today. So how do we continue to improve and excel?

Change your mindset from goal setting to setting standards. Standards are far more powerful than goals could ever be. Goals are something you hope to accomplish; standards are metrics you refuse to fall below. Which one is stronger? Goals are drawing a line in the sand of what you want to be. Standards are drawing the line in the sand behind you and refusing to cross back over it.

New Year's Resolution

Case in point. Have you ever had a goal to lose weight? Every January, the world is inundated with people who have New Year's Resolutions to lose X amount of pounds. With their new goal in mind, they set out on a quest to exercise and eat Healthy; to cross that line in the sand of being 20 pounds lighter. It goes without saying that the majority of people quickly forget about their goal within a few weeks. In fact, according to Amram Shapiro's "The Book of Odds: from lightning strikes to love at first site, the odds of everyday life," of those who actually make a New Year's resolution, only 1 in 8 people actually follow through with it.

Let's say you are in the small minority who stays committed to reaching your goal of weight loss. What often happens when you reach your goal weight? Celebration! After all you earned the right to have that piece of cheesecake or big meal that you've starved yourself from, right?! What happens slowly over time? Most end up back where they started or even bigger overtime and get caught in the cycle of dieting, gaining, dieting, and gaining again. Sounds familiar to a lot of us, right?

Why is it that we set these goals, accomplish them, and then revert back to who or how we were?

Usually the problem with goals is that the line in the sand we draw for them is a revolving door. You're allowed to cross the line, and you're allowed to go back across the line. Standards allow no such option. With the mindset of new standards for your life, you're thinking changes. You no longer hope you can lose 20 pounds. You KNOW that a healthy you is one that is 20 pounds lighter. It's who you are. With that mindset, what do you think happens when you get 20 pounds lighter? You stay there. The line in the sand is a one-way street, there's no turning back.

How much quicker do you think you'd get to whatever it is you're after if you draw that line behind you instead of in front of you? Instead of the next meal becoming your "last cheat meal" why not make the last cheat meal you had, your last one?

Setting that standard or setting that bar that you refuse to fall below is the most effective path to excellence. Rephrase that "goal" of yours right now with the mindset of a new standard. You're no longer "trying" to lose weight. You eat and exercise like a person at their goal weight.

Unlike goals, standards continually raise the bar. Goals are complacent. Standards are an ever-evolving bar, continuously rising, continuously challenging you to improve. Goals offer nothing left to do when you reach them because they are static benchmarks and metrics. Standards are ideals that are always progressing.

A goal may be to lose weight; a standard is a healthy way of life. A goal may be to spend 30 minutes with your family; a standard is a solid life/work balance. A goal may be to find a spouse; a standard is to become the perfect person for that spouse.

Those small changes in mindset can cause your life to travel in completely different places. We set goals simply because we think it will bring us happiness or fulfillment. Have you ever worked hard towards a goal, achieved it, and still felt empty afterwards? We all have. Why do you think that is? Most likely you mislabeled what it was you were really after. You chase a goal that you believe will bring a certain feeling and are left more defeated when it doesn't.

It happens all the time in relationships. How many times has someone asked you "what is your type" as if there are only a few components that make up most humans? You probably have friends who get sucked in to one bad relationship after the other because they always fall for the same "type." Most people in these cyclical toxic relationships are chasing the illusion of what they think they want, without ever asking themselves what it is they truly need.

Goals are what you chase, standards are who you are. Imagine if that same person, instead of chasing and adapting and conforming to be right for that "type" of person, took a standards approach to dating. What if they decided the characteristics they were looking for in a partner, and settled for nothing less than anyone who could be chivalrous, caring, loving, and all the great traits that a spouse should have? Don't you think their chances of finding a happy and everlasting relationship would be much higher? Of course. They set the standard.

When you set standards in your life, you're unwilling to budge or veer off course. In setting solid healthy standards, you move closer to excellence because you know what you stand for. If you just set goals, it's easy to lose sight of where you're going. That small veering off course can have far reaching implications of where you're trying to get to in life.

A Tale of Two Ships

Imagine two large boats leave the port of San Francisco, both headed for Tokyo, Japan. One boat is named Standards, and refuses to deviate from that course. The other boat, Goals, is willing to make a few changes if the waters get a little rough. The Standards' ship is willing to weather the storm and remain strong because it's focused on where it's going. The Goals' ship doesn't like storms or rough waters, so it deviates from the course just a tad, 1%. Over the numerous weeks it takes to cross the ocean, that 1% veering off course compounds and ultimately guess where that ship ends up landing?... Sydney, Australia!

That small change, in order to avoid the storms, caused the Goals to lose sight of where it was headed, and though it seemed to be on the right track, ended up in a completely different hemisphere. That happens to us in life if we don't set standards.

How many people do you know who live a life or have a job in an industry they absolutely despise because their "goal" a long time ago was to make money? How many people do you know in long term relationships where they despise one another but stay together because it was more "comfortable" than weathering the storms of being alone for a while? With no standard for what they were really after, they end up nowhere close to where they wanted to be.

BBM Me

In the early 2000s you couldn't look anywhere without seeing someone with a Blackberry phone. Blackberry was the clear standard of the business professional as it offered state of the art secure email and a revolutionary Blackberry Messenger that allowed you to securely speak with anyone across the world. To most of us, our BBM PIN was just as important as our phone number. Governments, Fortune 500 companies, and regular consumers flocked to join the Blackberry craze.

But something happened to Blackberry towards the end of the decade. Although they initially set a really high standard, Blackberry became complacent. They made the mistake of assuming that the bar was set so high that no one else could reach it. They forgot to raise the bar.

You have to understand when you set the new standard in anything, whether it be personal or professional, you attract competition. When you pursue excellence, you may currently be in the lead because of the bar you've raised, but you've now also become a target. It's all the more reason to keep pushing toward excellence, to keep growing, to keep innovating.

Blackberry failed to do all of the above. They made the fatal assumption that what they were doing was "good enough." Meanwhile, out in Cupertino, California, Steve Jobs worked on a new standard at the Apple headquarters. He didn't want a product that could compete with Blackberry, he wanted to completely revolutionize the way people used their phones.

In his keynote speech, the large blue screen showed a quote from Wayne Gretzky that said, "I don't skate to where the puck is, I skate to where it's going to be." With that said, Steve Jobs introduced the iPhone to the world. A fully touch screen device that did away with "pesky keyboards and trackballs" and offered full media and music capabilities, secure email and a whole lot more all in one device.

This was a deathblow to Blackberry. In that instant, everything changed. The new standard was set. People looked at their Blackberry phones and now saw a clunky device with a track pad that didn't work correctly and instantly longed for that sleek beautiful screen of an iPhone.

Steve Jobs said he never believed in doing focus groups. He said if you ask people what features they want, they'll tell you they want the things that are already out. With that mindset, you'll be chasing competitors your entire life. However, if you, like Apple, set the bar high based on a standard of quality and not how well you compare to everyone else, you'll likely be a leader and live an extraordinary life.

Over the next few years, Blackberry plummeted as businesses and consumers flocked to the iPhone. Do you think Apple got complacent with the new standard of what a phone should be? Absolutely not. As soon as it was released, Apple was hard at work creating a new iPhone so strong that the current iPhone would be obsolete. They competed only with themselves.

What did Blackberry do? They tried to create phones that had features and the look and feel of an iPhone. It failed as well.

When you focus on setting the standard, you're only in competition with yourself. Don't live your life based on what everyone else is doing. Set a standard of excellence based on what you know you're capable of doing. There are plenty of rabbits out there hopping around from one goal to the next, jumping all around life. Become the tortoise who is focused on one thing, the finish line. The tortoise didn't worry when others said how overmatched he was or how far ahead the rabbit seemed to be. The tortoise knew his path, knew what he could do, and stayed on the path he set for himself. We all learned as children, the tortoise always beats the hare. That's because the tortoise set a focused standard of consistency and the hare set an unfocused goal.

What standards are you willing to set right now in order reach the pinnacle of your life? Will those standards ensure that you get there? Standards are like train tracks, and if you're solid enough in setting them, you won't be derailed from your destination.

Chapter 4 – Excellent isn't Enough

From the second you hear the infectious bass line and the words "Yo VIP, let's kick it," followed by a whispered "ice ice baby," most people, fans of rap or not, can recite the words to Vanilla Ice's smash single, "Ice Ice Baby". The song received international acclaim, topped the charts in numerous countries, was featured in blockbuster movies, and launched the young Vanilla Ice to superstardom.

You couldn't watch a MTV show or turn on the radio in 1989 and not hear that song. The single itself went platinum and led his debut album, "To the Extreme", to sell over 15 million copies worldwide, becoming the fastest selling rap album of all time.

Vanilla Ice created an excellent song that almost everyone could sing along to as he basked in his worldwide fame throughout 1990.

In 1991, Ice learned a valuable lesson that we can all benefit from - one excellent feat does not equal excellence. Vanilla Ice, fresh off the album that sold over 15 million copies, released his next album a year later and it completely flopped. Entertainment Weekly called it one of the most ridiculous albums ever released.

Excellence is the ability to continually excel. It's easy to be excellent once. It's hard to be excellent daily. The pursuit of this is the essence of excellence.

Excellent work can make you successful overnight. You might win a case for your law firm, close a major deal with a new client, or lead your team to a championship, but can you repeat that daily? Success is the enemy of excellence because it lulls a lot of people into believing they will maintain that level of success without continuously striving to do better.

The lottery is a great example of this. People have a lucky night and pick an excellent set of numbers and win large sums of money, becoming richer than they could have ever dreamed. In one night, they make more money than they could possibly ever spend and live happily ever after, right? Wrong. According to a

2010 study by the University of Kentucky, Vanderbilt, and Pittsburgh, over 70% of lottery winners who come into unexpected large amounts of wealth are completely broke within 7 years of winning. That's an alarming statistic. That one excellent moment was not an indicator of a life of excellence.

In the world of sports, professional athletes do anything they can to get the edge on their competition. Unfortunately, many have now turned to performance-enhancing drugs, such as steroids, to boost their performance and give them excellent results. In the case with Major League baseball, these drugs aid in producing excellent record-setting seasons, but the cheating is almost always caught eventually.

That "quick fix" to have that miracle season has everlasting negative implications. In 1998, Mark McGwire set, at that time, the single season homerun record with 70 homeruns, an amazing accomplishment. But McGwire was eventually caught using steroids, and he, like many homerun records, now has an * next to his statistics, which will likely keep him out of the Hall of Fame (a true testament of excellence.)

The Ironman

On the other hand, you have Cal Ripken Jr., known by many as the Iron Man. Ripken Jr. played for the Baltimore Orioles for 21 seasons. His career included 19 All-Star appearances and 2 MVP awards, but what truly classified Cal Ripken as a man of excellence was his ability to break a 56-year-old record that many believed would never be broken. He broke the record for playing the most amount of games consecutively. For 17 years, 2,632 games, Ripken Jr. never missed a game. He voluntarily ended his record and took a night off. His career was built on consistency, a cornerstone of excellence. His accomplishments and records will likely never fall. He achieved that by improving himself mentally and physically every year, remaining healthy, and focusing on being the best third baseman he could be for the Baltimore Orioles. His excellence was rooted in his reliability and durability. Because of his continuous improvement and dedication to his team, he garnered a laundry list of awards and will forever be remembered in the Hall of Fame. There's no * next to the career of Cal Ripken Jr.

Excellent is a high point; excellence is a continual uphill slope. Focus on that. In all that you do, ask yourself, am I getting better daily? Am I putting myself in a position to improve daily? There should always be room for growth in your life. If you feel you've reached the top of your craft or your situation, either find a new way to raise the bar or find something new to do. Never stop growing. If you think you've reached the pinnacle of performance, perhaps you should rethink your growth. It might be that you need to take a step back and find a new way to grow to reach newer heights and increased longevity, as was the case with Tiger Woods after the 1997 Master's Golf Tournament.

Tiger Woods

The Masters, which brings all the top golfers in the world for a championship event, is likely the most prestigious golf tournament in the world. With all the competition, the margin for error is small. One bad shot and any golfer is likely out of contention for the win.

Did Tiger play a great game and squeak by with a win? No. He completely annihilated the competition. He won the tournament by a record 12 strokes! All of the best golfers in the world, playing at the same time, on the same course, came nowhere near Tiger's score, which was deemed a perfect tournament by many. It was the most excellent performance anyone had ever witnessed at the Masters. Tiger was clearly in a league of his own.

He could have continued to ride the momentum of that spectacular performance and relaxed, knowing he was hands down the best golfer in the world. Many would have, but not Tiger. Tiger did the unthinkable.

While watching his own performance, he didn't find one thing wrong with his swing. He found numerous things wrong with his swing! His swing was so bad, he thought, that it needed to be completely overhauled. What?!?! Here's a guy who had just won the greatest golf tournament by an unprecedented margin and he felt his swing needed to be completely revamped, not just tweaked.

Why do you think he felt that way? It's because Tiger Woods has a commitment to excellence, not just being excellent. Woods wanted to be consistently better, not just occasionally great. While others marveled at what he was currently doing, he looked at the bigger picture and what he wanted to accomplish. He felt his current swing would only get him so far. His goal was to be the best in the world for a long time so he stepped back and equipped himself with a swing that would allow him to do that. That's excellence at its finest!

Are you willing to analyze your finest moment and find areas of improvement or do you ride the wave of success while you have it? The answer to that question is a good indicator of what you value, excellence or simple success. Remember, consistent small steps always get you further than one giant leap.

Everyone knows somebody who lives in the past. We all have that friend who always reminds you of how good they "used to be" or the great things they used to do. Do you roll your eyes when they dive into their story of the "good old days?" If you have ever gone to a high school reunion, you most likely found many people reliving their glory days. If you looked around, you found the majority of the successful people are those you didn't necessarily remember. While many of the popular kids may have peaked in high school, having excellent athletic careers or whatever it may be, there were those who were working silently in the classroom. Day by day, they honed their skills and enhanced their knowledge. They weren't focused on being popular in school, they focused on pursuing a career they loved. Most of those types now go by another name, "boss." Those individuals caught in who they used to be have already peaked, and though they may have been excellent, they do not move towards excellence.

Remember, excellence has no end goal or peak point; it's a continuous improvement. The difference between being excellent and practicing excellence is one's ability to handle the pressure of setting the bar. Those who continually perform at heightened levels are those who achieve excellence. In sports, we call them "clutch." The guy who you can count on time and time again to hit the game winning shot or lead the game winning drive. In business, we call them closers. They always get the sell.

When you're consistently great at what you do, not everyone appreciates it. Your prevalence places a target on your back. You become the team to beat and everyone plays their best against you, or perhaps every other salesman in your company has the goal to unseat you as the head salesman. This can make or break most people. Some say they get "motivated" by the competition and it pushes them to do better. However, the truly great people don't worry about the competition and who's gunning for them. They are living to push their own standards. They are their own competition. People of excellence understand that the challenge they continually bring to themselves far outweighs the challenge anyone else could bring them.

The Strikeout King

Excellence often lies in the ability of not being afraid to fail. Too many people have an excellent season or sales period or whatever it may be and become crippled with the fear that they can't replicate those results consistently. Excellence concerns itself with nothing but giving the best effort.

George Herman Ruth, Jr. was a prime example of excellence. In 1923, he set a Major League Baseball record for homeruns in one season, hitting an astonishing 60 homeruns; a record that would stand for over three decades. George, better known as Babe Ruth, set another important and long-lasting record that year... strikeouts. That's right. In 1923, no one struck out more than Babe Ruth.

The secret to his excellence was the fact that he wasn't afraid to strikeout. He said, "Every strike brings me closer to my next homerun." He hit 60 homeruns that year and struck out 93 times. Most people don't achieve excellence because they let the fear of striking out in their profession keep them from stepping up to the plate.

Excellence is the ability to strikeout in life and get back up to the plate with the same confidence and tenacity as the last time, knowing your homerun is coming. Babe Ruth said he never heard boos on a homerun, but always heard them on a strikeout. He knew both went hand in hand, so he focused on the homerun.

Do you focus on the opportunity of what your hard work could bring, or are you hindered by the chance of failure?

Excellence isn't defined by those failures. It's defined by the improvements you make after those failures. Success via excellence, then, is the ability to climb on top of the mountain of failures until you reach your pinnacle.

This Sucks

Excellence isn't familiar with the term failure because it knows it by a different name, learning. Sir James Dyson got a crazy idea one day to create a vacuum that didn't lose suction when sucking up dirt, like the popular Hoover vacuum of the late 1970s did.

There are stories of people who had numerous failures that turned to successes such as Thomas Edison and the 1000 failures, or as he put it, 1000 steps, to create a working light bulb. However, Sir James Dyson's story takes the cake. From the time of his idea, Dyson worked for 15 years and used his entire life savings trying to bring his concept to life. He developed 5,126 prototypes… that didn't work.

He didn't worry about the "failures" because he said he learned something from each one. By learning, he was able to build momentum. Others saw failure, he saw progress. On the 5,127th try, the Dyson Vacuum was born.

At an estimated $4.5 billion dollars, Sir James Dyson and his industry-leading vacuum are proof of what happens when you focus on getting to where you know you could be and not worrying about the "failures" or obstacles that get in the way.

Excellence is an addictive trait. Learn to look at your perceived failures and find something in each one that you can learn from so that you improve next time. If you work hard enough and long enough and learn from each failure, by process of elimination, you'll achieve excellence.

Excellence is the ability to keep shooting toward a dream regardless of the outcome of each shot. Michael Jordan missed over 9,000 shots in his career of excellence, but no one talks about those. You know why?

Because in the end, if you hit the game winner, no one talks about all the shots you missed. Keep shooting.

Chapter 5 – Attitude of Excellence

Think about the last time you were around a great leader. Did their presence make you feel like you could accomplish anything? They most likely exhibited confidence, not only in themselves, but the team's ability to succeed. Because of their prevailing mindset, great results occur. This happens in businesses with powerful CEOs, it happens in wars with great generals, and it happens to elite sports franchises with outstanding coaches.

We often call this phenomenon that sets the greats apart from each other, the culture, whether it be the team or individual. The culture always trickles down from the top and reverberates throughout the organization. The culture is a reflection of the attitude of the person in charge.

I consult corporate clients on their digital strategy, often meeting with leaders and CEOs directly. It never fails; the first time I walk into a business, I look at two things which will determine if I take on the potential new client. First, I look at the body language of the employees. If everyone looks stressed, overworked, with no sense of fulfillment or happiness, I can tell you a lot about the leadership without even meeting upper management. When I do meet the CEO, the other criteria I examine is their attitude. Regardless of the type of business or the budget of the company, the attitude of those running it is a direct indicator of the future of that company. I've met bosses that had all of the right tools to be able to succeed. They had great products, a huge marketing budget, and plenty of manpower, yet I turned them down because their leadership style demonstrated the company' imminent failure If a bad precedent is set at the top, eventually it will sink the company.

On the other hand, I've walked into businesses that on paper, looked like they didn't have a chance in the world to make it out of the year. They may only have a decent product, little manpower, and not a big budget, but I would take on the client for one simple reason. The CEO truly believes in his company and his people.

Attitude dictates everything. *Excellence is a prevailing attitude of possibility.* Picture an attitude of excellence as a large ocean liner, perhaps a large aircraft carrier or an enormous ship. Though the ship is gargantuan in size, two things control its fate. The steering wheel and the anchor. One small turn of the steering wheel and the boat makes a large turn. With the drop of the anchor, the boat stays still. Your attitude should be that steering wheel and that anchor. Understand that small changes to your mindset have far reaching effects on your actions and future results.

Be careful which way you steer your mind because your life goes in the direction that you steer it. If you constantly turn away from adversity, or cower in fear at the thought of opposition, you'll spend your entire life in the bays and shallow waters of success. However, if you set a "full speed ahead, stop at nothing to get to the land of my potential" direction for your mind, your body will follow. It is people with that type of mindset who realize the real treasures of life are always in the deep uncharted waters.

Those with an attitude of excellence are never comfortable in their comfort zone. They view comfort as idle, and they instead prefer to push their limits. You must also control the anchor in your mind. Anchor your thoughts in a positive direction. When you do so, you're keeping your mindset in an unwavering direction. Remember, a helium balloon can only rise as high as the object it's anchored to. Your actions are like that balloon; no matter how high they wish to be, they are ultimately going in the direction of your attitude and thoughts. If you have a "sinking ship" mentality, then your actions and future will sink as well. If you have a "soar like an eagle" mindset, then your actions will know no limits. Make sure that your attitude sets its foundation on an escalator moving upward. When you do so, even the days when you take a step back, you'll still be moving up.

Do you operate with an attitude of excellence or an attitude of mediocrity? Earlier we defined excellence not by whether you see the glass half full or empty, but by how well you fill the glass.

Look, Opportunity!

Two salesmen for a great shoe company went overseas in search of new business. Both arrived at a new island, one day apart. On the island were thousands of natives, all of them barefoot and happy. The first salesman saw this and had a dejected look on his face and quickly boarded the boat back home, as he saw no opportunity. The second salesman, arriving a day later, looked at all the barefoot natives and instantly called his superiors and excitedly told them to send thousands of shoes! No one on this island had them. It was the perfect market!

What was the difference in these two men? Both had the exact same product, the exact same opportunity. In fact, the first salesman had the opportunity first. Yet he wasn't successful because his attitude didn't focus on what could be; he only saw what was. The other salesman, operating with an attitude of excellence, didn't look at the barefoot natives and sees the situation as hopeless. He saw nothing but opportunity.

Just because something currently is an accepted standard or way of life, doesn't mean your inspired action can't change that. We never view the world or people in it as they are. We view them based on how we are.

Find a Yes

Soichiro Honda embodies the attitude of excellence. Excellence is never quitting, even when conventional wisdom or the circumstances around you says that you should. As a young boy, Soichiro saw a Ford Model T car and was instantly hooked on the idea of the automobile, dreaming of one day making his own. After spending years as a mechanic, he started toward that dream by deciding to learn to make a solid piston ring to sell to Toyota to place in the engines of their cars. He spent years working on it, having to pawn his wife's jewelry for working capital until he finally created the perfect piston ring...or so he thought. He presented the ring to Toyota who told him his piston ring did not meet their standards. His dreams were dashed.

But he didn't quit. He went back to school to study more, all the while enduring the laughs and sneers of all the other engineers. He finally built a solid piston ring and received a contract to mass produce for Toyota, but there was one problem. Japan was going to war, and materials needed to make a factory to produce the rings were in short supply. If he had no factory, he could produce no products. As is the case with those who have an attitude of excellence, Honda found a way.

Building materials were scarce, so he created a new process to create building materials. He devised a way to create a new concrete building process and was able to build his factory. He was now ready to start producing piston rings except for the fact that his factory got bombed...twice. After rebuilding it, steel then became a scarcity. Though he found a way to get new materials, his factory was then destroyed by an earthquake.

To a person with a regular attitude, all signs would lead to quitting. Honda, knew what he could be and refused to allow himself to think that anything less would be acceptable. After the war, gasoline was in diminished supply, so the majority of Japanese began riding bicycles instead. Honda, seeing an opportunity, attached a small motor to a bicycle and created a motorized bike. He then repeated the process for neighbors and friends.

Seeing the potential of what the motorized bike could be, he wrote letters to the 18,000 bike shop owners asking them to help in his dream of rebuilding Japan via these motorized bikes. Five thousand shop owners sent him some money and he worked to create a small engine to make the motorized bike more practical. The bike sold well across the world.

He would later take his knowledge of a small engine and create small cars, which were a hit worldwide. It all started with an attitude of excellence and the anchored belief in Honda's ability and desire to one day create his own vehicle. When your vision is strong enough, you're willing to take any path to get there.

We all view the world through our own rose-colored glasses. Be sure your glasses are tinted toward advancement not complacency. Is your mindset strong enough to force you to do whatever it takes to advance in your life? Are you willing to build your factory, by any means necessary, as many times as necessary, in order to manufacture your dreams? Is your attitude anchored in an ever-improving escalator of possibility and opportunity?

Characteristics of the Excellence Attitude

So how do you develop an attitude of excellence? Each of us are unique, all with our own idiosyncrasies and mannerisms, however, an attitude of excellence always embodies four things.

Unwavering Belief in Self

People of excellence believe in themselves, even if they are the only ones that do. This belief doesn't come from conceit, but from the genuine thought that their initiative or purpose can impact the world in a positive manner. When you believe in yourself, you find a way to prosper. *True belief is jumping off a cliff knowing you'll figure out how to fly before you hit the ground.*

Silver Lining

There are always dark clouds on the road to anything worthwhile. Most people focus on the ominous clouds and the potential storms. Those of excellence focus on the silver lining. The silver lining around the edges of the dark cloud remind us that the sun is still shining and there are brighter days ahead.

When you develop an attitude of excellence, you look forward to adversity because you realized that great adversity opens the door to immense success. Do you concentrate on how dark or long the tunnel is or the light at the end? Excellence focuses on the light.

Persistence

Excellence doesn't focus on the length of the journey; it's about taking positive steps to reach the destination. You have to be willing to put your best foot forward, every day, not just on the days you feel like it. Anyone can have an excellent day when they feel like it. Excellence is reserved for those who continually move forward, regardless of that feeling. You are not deterred by losses in life, and you do not bask too long on your triumphs, but rather continue to improve, continue to excel, daily.

It's Never Good Enough

An attitude of excellence is happy because of the purpose being pursued, but is never content. You must view your life as a gradual slope of improvement, not a specific point to reach. Explore ways to better yourself and your life rather than just focusing on the destination. Learn to appreciate how far you've come, but keep your attention on how far you're capable of going and continue to move in that direction.

Remember, your attitude determines your steps. Be sure you're steering your thoughts down the path of excellence. It's on that path alone that marvels and true joys of life reside. We've now painted the picture of excellence and you should have an understanding and desire for excellence in your own life.

You are now ready to learn the qualities of excellence and begin to live a life of excellence yourself.

Here we go…

QUALITIES OF EXCELLENCE

Chapter 6 – Purpose

After reading five chapters filled with illustrations and examples that demonstrate why it's necessary to become the best you, you're probably asking yourself an important question.

How do I truly become a person of excellence? What are the steps?

First of all, there is no magic "how to guide", or any "follow these 10 steps and excellence is guaranteed" formula. Remember, excellence is an ideal. It's a constant pursuit of something better, not an end goal. That being said, there are five characteristics of excellence that 100% of men and women of excellence embody. If excellence is what you're truly after, you must focus on all five. You can become excellent with a few of them, but true excellence requires all five.

The first and foremost quality of excellence, and arguably the most important, is purpose.

Purpose is the passionate pursuit of an outcome that will extend past your existence.

Simply put, it has to be bigger than you. No one ever became legendary without having a legendary purpose. Purpose has turned ordinary men into immortal figures. A strong purpose of a few men has changed nations, defeated insurmountable odds, and created the world as we know it. Your purpose can be responsible for creating a better tomorrow.

The key to a solid purpose is to recognize that it has to be about more than just you. You can be the driving force behind it, but the beneficiary can't be limited to just yourself. By definition, the purpose you pursue has to extend past your lifetime. It has to be something so strong that others are willing to carry it on when you fall. It's an ideal, not an end goal.

A Famous Dream

Martin Luther King Jr. didn't just have a goal of getting to use the same restrooms, water fountains, and sit at the same restaurants as the whites. His purpose on earth was to create a world where race no longer mattered. In the mid-1900s, when he fought for that purpose, it would have seemed like a pipe dream. He knew it wasn't something he could accomplish in his lifetime, but his famous words "I have a dream, that one day…" echoed through the halls of eternity. His purpose was so strong that he got over 250,000 people to march to Washington D.C. to hear more about his purpose and his dream. This is way before the days of social sites and email or even the internet. His passion toward his purpose in life caught fire in the hearts and minds of others. His purpose is still being lived out today more than 50 years after his famous speech.

Why Have a Purpose?

Before the days of GPS and satellite, sailors sailing the oceans and travelers of the land all used the North Star to coordinate their location and their destination. The North Star was a constant; the one thing any traveler could always look up to, and know it would always be there.

Your purpose is that North Star. In all of your actions, and in everything you do as you navigate the ocean of life, you should look to it for guidance. You should ask yourself, am I moving toward this star?

The reason most people live in a land of mediocrity their entire lives is not that they don't have a purpose. It's that they never stopped to think about what it is. Imagine if those ancient sailors of the world had no North Star or guiding light. What do you think the likelihood of them reaching a destination would be? Sure, they may be able to cruise along in calm waters, but what happens when the storms of life toss and turn the boat?

We all get pushed around by the waves of life. What separates people with purpose and those without it is that we, those with purpose, can look to it and correct our path while those without it simply just float in the direction they're headed. Seems illogical to not have a purpose then, right?

When Should I Develop My Purpose?

Now is the best time to develop and hone in on your purpose. In Q&A sessions with audiences, I often find that most people think they are too young to develop their purpose, and unfortunately, some feel they are too old to develop one, as if purpose is a boat or a bus that, if you miss it, your chance is over.

Pursuing your purpose isn't about the number of years you spend on it, rather, it is the quality of the time you spend pursuing it. Don't estimate the power of passion if you feel you're too old and don't underestimate the power of purpose if you feel you are too young to get anything accomplished.

Nelson Mandela was a strong advocate of democracy and the need to eliminate racism in his native South Africa. He believed in the equality of all people and would stop at nothing to see it through, despite living in a country opposed to his beliefs. At the age of 45 he was arrested and thrown in prison for his beliefs, which went against the laws in South Africa.

Imagine if Nelson Mandela let his false imprisonment burnout his North Star? Instead, Mandela stayed true to his purpose. He continued to write, learn, and lead from inside the prison walls. Nearly 27 years later, Mandela was released, and at the age of 72, continued his purpose and his dream of equality in South Africa.

Mandela would go on to become president of South Africa, as well as a world renowned figure for his non-violent, driven approach. South Africa, as a result of Mandela's purpose and liberation movements, has freed all its people. All of this from a man who refused to let his purpose die despite the situation and circumstances.

Remember, if your purpose is strong enough and bright enough, no amount of dark clouds or adverse situations can prevent you from keeping an eye on it.

How Do You Determine Your Purpose?

Finding your purpose is as simple or complicated as answering the following question - Why?

Why do you wake up every morning? Why did you choose your partner? Why do you work for a living? Why are you here on earth?

Why is the single greatest question we can ask ourselves. In answering the question, our whole lives can become more focused and powerful. We've seen examples of what happens when ordinary men burn with passion in pursuit of their purpose.

We all have that purpose inside of us. Many of us just don't know where to look or what to look for. When you were younger, perhaps you played the picture storybook game "Where's Waldo?" You knew two things for sure — 1) Waldo was hidden somewhere on the page and 2) He always wore the same red & white striped sweater. Finding him then was a matter of careful focus and patience.

Your purpose is a lot like that. Two things are for certain — 1) It exists, waiting to be found and 2) It always encourages consistent action.

Let's look at how we can find our purpose.

What Do You Enjoy?

I'm not concerned with what puts a small smile on your face. Ask yourself, what do you TRULY enjoy? What puts a smile in your soul and gives you an uncontrollable sense of happiness and peace? Is it a walk through nature? Is it watching your kids or grandkids grow up? Is it a business idea that you can see revolutionizing the entire world?

Think about your passions in life. All of us have a few. You might have a genuine love and appreciation for all types of music, art, or fashion. You might love science or religion or perhaps you love models of effective leadership or political structure. There is no right or wrong passion. What matters is that it's something that truly inspires YOU, not what you're told to be inspired by.

Don't get caught up in the dead end road of pretending to like, or psyching yourself into liking something because you're afraid others won't understand or will think your passion is stupid. Don't think your passion isn't valid because it doesn't seem profitable or worthwhile. Purpose is never about finances, and no matter what it is you love, there are millions of people who love the exact same thing. Besides, even if it was about money, there has never been an industry or passion in the history of the world that hasn't made someone a millionaire. Most likely the person was so passionate about it that they focused on the purpose and the financial success followed.

Your passion should be yours alone, independent from the thoughts and opinions of others. It can be as broad as space or as finite as eco-friendly paper bags. It just has to make your heart beat when you think about it.

Spend some time right now, or over the next few days or weeks, making a list of things that truly get your heart pumping and put a smile on your face. An easy way to start this list is to think about the last few times you were truly happy. The last times you laughed uncontrollably, smiled so hard your cheeks cramped, or felt such a sense of peace that you never wanted the moment to end.

How Much Do You Love It?

The answer to this question will help you drill down closer to your passion. It will separate your likes (hobbies) from loves (potential purposes). Scrolling through your list of joys, ask yourself, what would you do if that joy was taken away from you, permanently? Is it something you could live without, or is it something you would die without?

If you can't find something you couldn't fathom living without, then you need to expand your list, and that's ok! The goal is to find your purpose. There is no shot clock or time limit on how long it takes you. The journey is as important as the result. When you narrow it down to the few things you can't live without, ask yourself this - what would happen if that passion was taken away from the world, not just you?

If it's a true passion of yours, your heart no doubt just sank at the thought of that or perhaps you instantly got fired up in defending said cause. Good, you're closer to finding that passion.

A purpose is something you can't imagine the world not having. If you're an advocate of nature, you can't imagine a world without rainforests and beautiful rivers. If it is people you love, you can't imagine a world with people held against their will, forced to do what they don't want to do.

It has to be bigger than you, and you have to love it. Do you love your passion enough that if you were asked to spend the rest of your days improving or fighting for it, you wouldn't grow tired or want to quit? It's important to remember your purpose doesn't have to be something as heroic sounding as freeing slaves, or saving every species of wildlife, or other causes we see on every infomercial on television. It simply has to mean enough to you.

For every passion there is a purpose, for every true purpose passionately pursued, there is a benefit to society.

What Are You Willing to Do to See It Flourish?

You've found some things you love. You've drilled down into things that you are passionate about and couldn't live without, now the next question. What are you willing to do to see your cause continue? If you have a business that provides jobs and serves the community, what are you willing to do to make sure it thrives? If your children are your passion, what are you willing to do to provide them with the best opportunities in life? If it's a cause such as saving the rainforest, what are you willing to do to make the world go green?

If the answer to these questions isn't enough to make you even get off the couch, then you should start back at square one. I promise you, your purpose is hiding there somewhere, just like Waldo. When these questions start to resonate with you, you're on the right path. What are you willing to do? What are you not willing to let happen? If you care about the environment, will you let someone liter right in front of you? If you care about the growth of your business, will you allow your employees or co-workers to give a half-hearted effort?

How bad do you want it? Your purpose should mean so much to you that you can taste it. Excellence is an ideal that we chase, but our purpose should be clear, sharp, and focused in our mind. Too many people view their purpose on one of those old black & white TV's with the fuzzy gray channels and the long rabbit antenna ears. It's murky and fades in and out. A true purpose is seen in high definition with razor sharp focus.

If you were to spread your passion around the world, what would the world look like? Do you see smiles on the faces of the world all in high-definition? The thought of putting the same level of fulfillment and happiness into everyone in the world should start to move you! If it does, you're getting closer.

Does It Make You Take Immediate Action?

The final step in finding your purpose is asking yourself, does it make you take immediate action? If it's truly your purpose, you don't even have to ask yourself that question because the thought of what the world could be if your purpose was shared has already driven you into action.

Excellence is a series of steps that moves us along the path of our purpose. Everyday should be an immediate action in that direction. A true sense of purpose doesn't focus on the "how" but rather the "now." You don't have to know how you'll win the battle. You just have to be able to start the journey knowing you have what it takes to win the war.

If you're sprinting to battle right now, congratulations! You have found your purpose, and you are on the way to excellence.

Chapter 7 – Drive

You most likely remember that one of the first books you read as a child was about a little blue engine. The train, much smaller than the other large powerful trains, was given a task that the others passed on because of the degree of difficulty, to take a load over a steep mountain.

The little train focused not on the seemingly impossible task at hand, but on his own capabilities. He uttered the phrase "I think I can, I think I can", until it became an "I knew I could" reality.

"The Little Engine That Could" is a perfect example of potential when you possess the second quality of excellence, drive.

Drive is an unwavering advancement toward an ideal.

You may have heard it called by other names, "what makes you tick," "what motivates you," "what propels or powers you?" They all mean one thing - what drives you?

Drive is a quality that only you can fuel. We talked earlier about being solar powered versus gas powered, the former being an unlimited supply of energy. When your purpose is strong and clear enough, you'll realize it is the fuel that powers your vehicle. The path you take with that fuel is your drive.

Have you ever met someone that just "has it?" You see it all the time in small sports stars who play as if they're giants. You have heard about it in the famous story of David vs. Goliath. Whether it be man versus giant, or man versus machine, some people seem to be born with "the chip on their shoulder." It's almost as if their engine is bigger than the body it's housed in. Do you ever wonder why that is?

These select few individuals learned a lesson that most never do. The lesson is simply this - the engine that pushes you forward isn't limited to the size of your body or the appearance of your circumstances. People who exhibit this extreme drive don't fuel themselves based on a destination. They fuel themselves for a lifelong journey. They understand their tank has to stay full and when it runs low, they have to refill it.

Too many people are fine getting by with "just enough gas." Have you ever traveled with a friend or family member who always seems to have the "low gas" gauge on? Their response is always the same when asked why they don't fill up - "I have enough" to get me where I need to go. Most people operate their life in the same manner. They wake up and fuel themselves with just enough energy to make it through the day, or give just enough effort to not get fired or not get broken up with in a relationship. Do you think the "just enoughers" ever live a life of excellence? Absolutely not.

Why not? Because they fill their tanks with enough for the task at hand. What ultimately happens to them when something they didn't prepare for such as a detour or traffic enters their path? They run out of gas. Short-sighted thinking always gets you the short end of the stick.

On the other hand, those with strong drive, those men and women of excellence who understand the journey is a long one and the destination is far away, fuel themselves for that journey. They are prepared for everything. Regardless of the amount of time it takes to get to the land of excellence, no matter what obstacles, detours, or setbacks they may endure, one thing is for certain — they will not run out of gas.

If you've read the up to this point, then you too are one of those people with a full tank. If you currently don't have a full tank here's a little secret - you have the ability to fill your own tank. Think of it as a free gas card. If you had a free gas card, would you not keep your tank full?

Your purpose should be so vivid that you'll stop at nothing to get there. That's a good thing because those with strong drive or will don't have brakes. The fast lane in life has three possible endings. You crash, you run out of gas, or you reach your destination. There is no off ramp to those with a strong purpose. Though you may crash on your path to excellence, it will not deter you from pushing forward to your destination. We've already established that you have the ability to fill your own tank, so running out of gas isn't an option. That leaves us with the last option — reaching our pinnacle, achieving excellence, fulfilling our purpose.

Why is Drive Important?

Drive is essential for men and women of excellence because it's you taking control of your present and future. Without it, you're simply a passenger on the ship of life, heading whatever direction life takes you. In case you're wondering, it never floats along to where you want to go. In fact, life is a lot like water. It flows in the direction that's most convenient, not the direction that's best for you. Rain falls from the sky and immediately heads downstream. Your purpose is to reach the top of the mountain. Life's direction is to flow downward.

Not only does it flow down the mountain, water is designed to filter into a larger body of water, the ocean of mediocrity. Scary isn't it? Still knowing that, most people are happy riding the lazy river of life because it's easier to complain than it is to change directions.

How many people do you know who could be labeled professional complainers? You hear it daily "oh my boss hates me," "oh my wife treats me so terribly," "oh it's not fair that Jim got the promotion and I didn't," the list goes on and on. You'll notice these men of mediocrity all have one thing in common; it's never THEIR fault. It's always the economy or the boss or the spouse or some other circumstance. Riding in the passenger seat of life will always get you downhill results. You may start at the top of the mountain, but you ultimately end up swallowed by the ocean.

Men of excellence go against the grain. Women of excellence grab the steering wheel in life and change direction. If you've been a serial complainer, riding in the passenger seat of life until now, it's okay. Grab the reigns right now and jump in the driver's seat of your own life.

Most can't do this because to do so would be admitting they have been slacking in their life thus far. However true that may be, it's much better to realize that now and correct it, than for your life to throw you off a cliff where there's no turning back.

Excellence is taking responsibility for your current situation. Once you accept your seat on the driver's side and put your hands on the wheel of your own life, you'll notice a sense of empowerment. You should, after all you're taking control of your own life! If you see the North Star, known as your purpose, in the rearview, simply turn around. No matter where you're at, change directions until you face your purpose….and hit the gas!

More importantly, when you hit the gas, don't let up. Drive is an UNWAVERING pursuit. Quitting or stopping are not options, regardless of how hard the terrain is you must cross.

How to Develop Drive?

There are four steps you need to take in order to develop and maintain drive on your journey to excellence.

Figure Out Where You Are

The number one mistake driven, or goal-oriented people make, is not knowing where they currently are. You can have the best destination in the world, but if you don't know where point A is, how can you ever get to point B? Think about the last time you used a GPS. The first question it asks you is your destination, correct? Then it asks you for your starting point. What happens if you don't fill in both sections? You get no map, no guidance or suggestions.

To develop a strong drive, you have to be blatantly honest with yourself about your current location in life. Includes acknowledging your positive traits, characteristics and relationships as well as the flaws, mistakes, and toxic situations you've placed yourself in. By ignoring the negative, you're giving yourself incorrect coordinates that will ultimately keep you off the path of your purpose. Any path can be corrected if you're willing to perform an accurate assessment of where you truly are. This is a benchmark that separates those of excellence, from those of mediocrity.

Reassess Where You're Going

It's not easy admitting our flaws to ourselves, or taking responsibility for the fact we may have allowed ourselves to go down the wrong path for far too long. I get it. Sometimes life knocks you sideways and you lose your sense of direction. The good thing about realizing where you're at is that life doesn't require you to make a 180-degree turn while going full speed. That's a recipe for disaster.

After realizing where you are, don't think that you have to instantly spin around. Pull off to the side of the road and envision your purpose. The storms of life don't last forever. When they clear, look back at your star. Take out the photo of the children who you love so much. Look back at the mission statement you created for your new business, or think about that vow you made to your partner. Often, this not only reminds us why we set out on this path, but it also refills our tank.

Once you realign where you're going with where you are, hit the gas.

Read the Dash

The dash of a vehicle operates much like the human body. When all things are good, it's relatively quiet. When something isn't right, it sends us signals. Our body says "ouch this hurts," a vehicle says "check engine." There are always signals.

Listen to them. A car dash may have signals for wiper fluid, tire pressure, or the engine. In the same manner, you need to make sure that you have gauges that check things that matter — your own engine, your loved ones, and a compass for your direction.

The first step is to make sure that you're happy and fulfilled. It might not be all days of smiles, but you should rest at night knowing your progress moved you closer to your purpose and you gave your all to it. *True happiness is the attainment of daily fulfillment.* Are you keeping your tank full? Are you operating at maximum capacity physically, emotionally, mentally, and spiritually? If not, what needs to be done to fix it? Remember, it's better to slow down and fix a problem than it is to deal with a catastrophe. You can afford to slow down and tune your engine. You can't afford to have to replace the entire engine. Listen to yourself and read the signs.

Secondly, listen to those you care about. Remember, purpose is about more than just you, so make sure you're not neglecting those on the journey with you. If you've ever taken a family road trip, then you understand everyone has different needs at different times. Some can be ignored, but others have to be adhered to. You, as the captain of the ship, whether it be the CEO of a business or head of the household, are responsible for those in your care. Be sure their needs are met. After all, this whole journey is about them anyway, isn't it?

Finally, periodically check and make sure you're headed in the right direction. Sometimes we get blinded by a sense of pride which tells us "we know a better path." Your purpose is that star that consistently stays in the same spot. Be sure you're headed towards it at all times.

Look for Signs and Landmarks

Though excellence is an ideal and purpose is something that outlives us, it's important to make sure you are progressing. Too often people drive in circles, or even worse, spin their wheels in place and never progress in life.

There's a difference in being busy and being productive. I learned that valuable lesson when I began taking swimming lessons in pursuit of becoming an Ironman Triathlete. I thought by flailing my arms frantically at the water, somehow I would move quickly like some sort of 6'4 spastic shark. After what seemed like an eternity in that training session, I looked up to see that not only had I not progressed, I actually floated backward. Busy does not mean productive. I learned smooth, calm, efficient strokes bring better results than splashing the water hard.

While in the pool, my swim coach told me that someone who splashes around and doesn't move is known as a "funny YouTube Video waiting to be seen," but in the ocean where many Ironman swims take place, it's known by another name, "bait." Lesson learned.

In the same manner, make sure you're not simply treading water or splashing in place. There's nothing wrong with having metrics, or landmarks so to speak, to make sure that you are indeed progressing. If you make the mistake of working "hard" but not in an effective manner, you eventually will get tired and stop. However, if you see you're making progress, you'll find the intestinal fortitude to continue on towards excellence and the fulfillment of purpose.

Keep that "I think I can" mantra until you reach the point of "I knew I could" and then set your sights even further up the road. Drive on toward excellence.

Chapter 8 – Habit

I was once asked by a very successful businessman what my goal was. I replied, like all young entrepreneurs, "I want to make a million dollars." Assuming he'd be impressed with my "aspirations," he sat there and shook his head quietly, and told me he'd tell me the secret to getting that million dollars.

I leaned in, obviously excited to know the secret that had made him a millionaire hundreds of times over. I expected to get a life changing secret that I could keep to myself and repeat with all of my "businesses" (also known as my crazy ideas that I had somehow convinced myself I was the CEO of each) and would go on to make the Forbes list as a young 20-something year old and buy yachts, planes and mansions. It's the American dream, right?

I assumed the secret would be some special, elite network that I was about to be invited to, or some crazy stock I was about to receive insider trading on or some get rich quick idea that he was about to reveal because I impressed him with my "ambition."

I remember leaving that meeting dejected. What a stupid answer. It wasn't a magic formula. It wasn't a "get rich quick" idea. It wasn't even a secret. It was dumb. Or so I thought. The secret, he said, to making a million dollars was this two-step process:

1. Find a way to make a dollar profit and make your first dollar.

2. Repeat that process 1,000,000 times.

STUPID! I was pissed. Duh, of course if I made one dollar a million times, I'd be a millionaire, but who would want to do that? That took consistency and a whole lot of hard work!

It wasn't until years later that I understood the parable of what he was trying to teach me. Yes, success is hard work, but lasting success in anything is about creating positive habits, the next quality of excellence.

Habits are a consistent sequence or process that marries you to your purpose daily.

In simpler terms, habits are actions you take every single day to move you closer toward fulfilling your purpose.

The more I study the excellence of legendary people, both past and present, the more I realize how important setting solid habits is. Habits are a tool to help you achieve your purpose. Therefore, it's important to know your purpose before you start setting good habits. Excellence is almost robotic. It's a repetition of a series of actions over and over. A million one dollar bills makes you a millionaire. Exercising and eating right to lose 2 pounds a week will help you lose 20 pounds in only 2.5 months. Regardless of your path, having consistent actions is the only way to get there. We've said it before, but the tortoise only beat the hare because he took consistent steps toward his goal, without hesitation or failure.

I stress to you the importance of forming good habits because it's equally as easy to form bad ones The problem with bad habits is that most people find ways to mask them. People who are habitually late find someone or something to blame, "traffic, parking, car trouble", every day. Those who are overweight always blame "fast food being cheaper, more convenient, etc." They never look at their own potentially lazy habits of sleeping in, or their terrible eating habits that created the excess weight. Poor habits mask themselves as "victim of circumstances." Again, it's easier to float down the mountain; therefore, it's easier to latch on to bad habits than productive ones.

How to Define Habits

Think about the habits in your life. Are they moving you forward? Here's a way to identify your current habits.

Monitor Your Time

For a period of two weeks, monitor everything you do, down to the minute. Be very specific. Don't just say 9-noon – work; break it down. From 9:00-9:17 am, surfed Facebook. From 9:17-9:23 am, walked around and chatted with other employees.

Just as the case with developing your drive, you have to understand where you are. NO matter who you are, you'll undoubtedly find that you spend a large amount of time doing things that aren't the most productive to where you want to go. It's okay as long as you recognize this with the intent to fix it.

Weed Out the Unproductive

At the time that this book was written, the number one bad habit for most people was spending too much time on social site or browsing the internet aimlessly. When you're looking at your list, highlight the things that you seem to do every single day that aren't 100% productive. Are you starting to see a pattern emerge? Time wasted with bad habits could be spent pursuing your purpose. Start by identifying one or two bad habits that waste a lot of time.

Notice I said start with one or two bad habits. Too many people work hard trying to radically change their lives overnight, instead of focusing on improving a habit or two at a time. Remember, a habit is something that you do unconsciously. Until it becomes habit, you have to train your mind and/or body to do it for roughly three weeks. You can't overload your system by making radical changes. However, you're more likely to succeed by changing a habit or two at a time until it becomes subconscious activity. Then move on to new habits.

Replace with Good Habits

For every bad habit you wish to change, it must be replaced with a good habit. First, decide which good habits will move you closer to your purpose. Next, assign one good habit to each of your bad habits. Let the bad habit trigger the good habit. If you're about to spend the next 15 minutes on Facebook or browsing the internet, substitute it instead with 15 minutes reading a book that will help you learn more about the industry you're in or the business you'd like to start. If you eat when you're nervous, swap out the chips and cookies with fruits and veggies. Three weeks is all it takes. Isn't it worth it to push through breaking bad habits and replacing them with good ones, all for the sake of moving towards your purpose?

Habits of Excellence

A creature of good habit is a creature of excellence. Anything you're willing to do daily that moves you closer to fulfilling your purpose, can be turned into a great habit. However, if you're unsure about which good habits to start with, here are some good some examples that people of excellence often possess.

Consistent Wake Up Time

You may think that you're an anomaly; that can sleep in late and "catch up", but the reality is that for the vast majority of icons from the past as well as the present, wake up extremely early, every day. After all, if your purpose means enough to you, you can't wait to hit the ground running towards it every day.

Learning

Excellence is a continual pursuit that requires knowledge. The further you go, the more knowledge you'll need. People of excellence set aside time daily to learn. It may come via reading a book, listening to an audiotape, or having lunch with a mentor. Learning from others' mistakes is the quickest way to save yourself the time and energy of making them yourself.

Become Decisive

How many times has someone asked you "where do you want to eat?" or "what do you want to do?" and you replied, "I don't know, what do you want to do?" We may see that as being friendly or polite, but true men of excellence are decisive. They know what they want because they know where they are headed. Answer questions in a direct manner that gets you closer to where you're trying to go. Realize that many people are afraid to answer because they don't want to be the one responsible for making a wrong decision. Excellence doesn't concern itself with that. Excellence is purpose-driven, not mistake-ridden.

Point Fingers at Yourself

Retire from the blame game. If you did something wrong, claim it. If your employee did something wrong, fault yourself for not teaching them correctly. If a relationship is on the rocks, figure out what you're doing to cause it to be that way. This isn't a self-depreciating path to depression. This is hinged on the fact that, if you take responsibility for how things are, you have the opportunity to change them. People respect a man who is not afraid to take the blame. That man ultimately gets credited with the rewards as well.

Exercise

It takes so little time, yet it's the one thing most people neglect. People living a life of mediocrity often claim they have "no time" to exercise. Yet, the CEOs, and other people of excellence, find the time to exercise and run the company. If they can do it, why can't you? Your body is a vehicle to get you to your dreams and aspirations. It can't get there if it's broken down. Maintain your body and keep it in great shape by exercising daily, so it can give you its best in return.

Head One Direction

You probably know someone, if not, then you might be that someone, who has a million different ideas and seems to wear a million different hats. *True excellence is having one singular focus.* If your daily actions are scattered and you're hopping around like a rabbit, you can't expect life to move in your favor. One completed task always beats 50 halfway-completed tasks. Complete a project and then move on to the next one. If you're balancing several things, find a way to align them. For instance, if you're strapped for time, find a way to exercise with the family. If you have several businesses, find a way to align them to work with each other. Move one direction.

How to Develop Great Habits

It's imperative to create and stick with great habits if excellence is truly what you're after. They may be some aforementioned habits, or you may have your own habits that you believe are a better fit for your purpose. Perhaps you know what you need to do, but aren't quite sure how to develop it. Here are a couple of tips that will allow you to create great habits using the Idea of Excellence M.E.R.I.T. formula.

Measure

Think of the habit you'd like to successfully employ and set small measurable goals toward attaining it.

Evolve

You may be ahead or behind on your steps toward attaining your habit. It's better to make small adjustments toward the measurable steps than to quit all together.

Review

Set benchmarks to stop and review your progress. If you're far behind, figure out what you need to do to get back on track. If you're farther ahead than you thought, instead of easing up, set new measurable goals that you can work toward.

Improve

Reward yourself by acknowledging your progress. Our bodies and minds love rewards. Find a reward that keeps you aligned with your purpose as you reach certain milestones in your path to creating good habits.

Teach

Accountability is the father of consistent change. Once you have mastered a habit, pass it on to another. Hold them accountable, and in the same manner, you'll keep yourself accountable to the new habit.

Let's say your goal is to start a habit of waking up at 5:00 am instead of 6:30 am and you're using the MERIT System. You have a 3-week goal to get to 5:00 am and you decide you will wake up 30 minutes earlier each week. Four days into the first week, you realize you're dragging at work and 30 minutes was too much to wake up early.

Therefore, you evolve your goal, scale it back, and wake up at 6:15 am the rest of the first week. After a few days you get the hang of waking up at 6:15 am and you review your goal. You know you need to be at 5:30 am based on your plan, but you realize it may not be viable. Instead of a 3-week plan of waking up 30 minutes earlier each week, you decide a 6-week plan of waking up 15 minutes earlier each week is more likely to work for you.

In your review, you set a metric to reward yourself when you reach the halfway point or 5:45 am. When you successfully wake up at 5:45 am, treat yourself to a nice breakfast, perhaps at your favorite diner, or take that long, relaxing bath. Something small that allows you to tell yourself "I am improving."

Finally, once you reach your goal of waking up at 5:00 am and it becomes a habit, help someone else along. Over time, you'll have enough people also waking up early to have a breakfast club or morning basketball game, all with the time you saved by not sleeping in.

Habits lead to results 100% of the time. It's up to you the type of habits you set because the results will be a byproduct of those habits.

Chapter 9 — Self-Control

There's an old Cherokee lesson about a grandfather speaking to his grandson. He tells his grandson "there's a terrible fight going on inside me, a fight between two wolves. One is evil – full of self-hate, ego, pride, guilt, resentment, laziness, envy, and jealousy. The other is good – full of love, compassion, truth, faith, honesty, and benevolence. This fight is going on inside you and every other human, too."

The boy asked, "Which wolf wins?"

The Old Cherokee responded with, "Whichever one you feed."

We all have forces of good that propel us to accomplish great things and we also have those voices of worry and self-doubt. Ultimately, only one side can prevail, but you control which side that is by which you decide to feed.

Self-control is the next quality necessary for excellence.

Self-Control are the actions that demonstrate the importance of the objective over the impulse.

Are you willing to turn down things that sound good right now in order to get things that you would like one day? Are you willing to turn down that piece of late night pizza in order to get the beach body you've always dreamed of? Are you willing to skip a weekend vacation with friends in order to work on that business plan? Are you willing to give up what you like in order to get the things you love?

Are you willing to give up the things you love in order to get the things you couldn't live without?

Your answer isn't dictated by words; it's dictated by your actions. What do your actions say about you? You say you'd like to get ahead in your career, yet your actions value those 30 minutes of hitting the snooze. You may say your new business idea could change your family's life, but you'd rather catch the newest blockbuster movie on a Friday than work towards it. Your actions always reveal the truth of what you say is important.

Self-control is about keeping your focus on where you're going and moving in an effective manner to get there. Too often, people have great goals, or great purposes, yet never achieve excellence because of the manner in which they attack that which they wish to achieve. How many horrific images have you seen in your life of the fastest sports cars wrapped around a tree or a pole because they lost control? Was it the car's fault? No. It had the capability to get from point A to point B. The problem was most often the driver, who pushed the car past its limits.

Always remember, just because the vehicle you're in (whether that be a company, a relationship, etc.) has the ability to go faster, doesn't mean you have to. No matter what the scenario is, when we go too fast, we make mistakes. In a vehicle traveling at a high rate of speed, a small twitch of the steering wheel can have catastrophic results.

Control is about mastering yourself, not others.

On the other hand, those who truly master themselves, achieve excellence. You must fully understand yourself so that you can adapt to your surroundings and still get the results you're after. There is perhaps no greater example of this than the martial arts master Bruce Lee.

Like Water

Bruce Lee grew tired of the stiff fighting routines of traditional martial arts. He found them to be unrealistic in real fights and yearned to find a way to teach true, real world self-defense.

While meditating on a boat, he grew frustrated with the thought of his past trainings and punched the water in defiance. He learned something valuable with that punch. The water was not affected by his punch.

He learned that water is never worried because water knows what it is. If you pour it in a glass, it takes the shape of the glass, yet it is still water. Bruce Lee would adopt this "formlessness" in his fighting. The focus then became less about trying to be something and more about getting the intended result.

Self-control pushes us to get results. It's not based on ego in trying to prove who or what we are, but by selflessly putting aside our pride to fulfill our desired purpose. Bruce made it clear why you should focus on what you're accomplishing versus getting caught up in the false pride says, "the stiffest trees are the most easily cracked, while the bamboo will survive by bending with the wind."

Are you content with who you are to the point where you don't feel the need to prove yourself to others? We often lose control when our pride dictates our actions, not our purpose. Water, in all its glory, is so simple and so serene, yet can wipe out cities when enough pressure is built up. You must maintain the same calmness of a beautiful ocean day because your power is tied to your purpose. You can't get caught up in proving your ability to destroy cities or create hurricanes or else you risk finding yourself spinning out of control in all the wrong directions, instead of following the stream of your purpose.

The hardest person to ever control is yourself. Insecurity (the opposite of excellence) is the intense desire to control others. You may have a boss, whom everyone knows isn't worthy of his position, go above and beyond to prove his power by boasting his title. You may have been in a relationship, or witnessed a time where one party tried to control the other party. The need to control others stems from the inability to control one's self.

Excellence is learning how to control yourself.

Why Should We Control Ourselves?

The simple answer is that you don't have time to waste if you're passionate about your purpose. Gravity shows us it's easier to be brought down than to be picked up. Undoubtedly, as you rise towards your purpose, there are those forces of mediocrity that will prefer that you stay the same. They will doubt you. They will provoke you and they will hurl insults your way. They'll try anything they can to get you to give up on your purpose because they're afraid to journey toward their own purpose.

You have a limited amount of time to unleash an unlimited amount of potential. Spend that time wisely. If you were in Los Angeles and your goal was to make it to New York, would you zigzag all over the country listening to everyone else's opinion on what the best city is? Would you stop in a town to prove to others that you were "on your way" to your dream? Sounds silly, doesn't it?

Yet many of us do it. Haven't we all been caught in the trap of proving something to someone as if that validation makes us any better or gets us any closer to our goal? Self-control is having the ability to block out what others want you to do because your internal voice knows what you need to do. It's about proving your self-worth to your purpose, not people.

How to Gain Self-Control

Discover Your Redlining Characteristics

Red is the color of passion. Red can be the color of love or the color of anger. When it comes to vehicles, redlining is pushing your car to the max. By the same token, when pushing your life to the edge, you have the power to propel or destroy yourself. With that much power, it's important to identify whether you are helping or hurting yourself. Do you have a short fuse? Do you anger easily? Do you lose your patience very quickly? What are the traits that take you from having a great day to fuming in anger? It's important to identify these so that we prevent ourselves from spiraling out of control by being blinded by this sea of red.

Know Your Limits

Remember, self-control is knowing yourself. Part of knowing yourself is knowing the triggers that force you to spiral out of control. Look at the list of your redlining characteristics and spend some time thinking about where the line is. Identify the line that once you cross it, you act out of character. If someone is twenty minutes late to a meeting, do you blow up in frustration? If a certain topic is discussed, do you lose yourself? Find out what lines turn you from a normal person into the Incredible Hulk.

Set Parameters for Yourself

If you know the actions or situations that cause you to lose your cool, set parameters and protocols that allow you to deal with them effectively. Focus on your purpose. If you know someone's tardiness to a meeting causes you to lose your temper, remind yourself that the said person might be late, but your anger and hostility towards that person won't move you any closer to your purpose. The goal is forward-moving strokes, not flailing around punching the water.

Remember What You're About

Your life is dedicated to pursuing a purpose, not detracting from the lives of others. Remind yourself of your purpose every day. Aside from keeping you focused on what matters, this simple task will save you time by avoiding things that don't move you toward that purpose. Conscious reminders of what you're after go a long way in declining opportunities or setbacks that won't get you there. If your purpose is to remain healthy in order to be there for your loved ones, and every day at 11:30 am you look at pictures of your family, most likely, you'll maintain the self-control needed to avoid binging at lunch. If your purpose is to rise up the ranks in your company to steer it in a direction that can more positively impact the world, get to work a few minutes early and walk down the halls of upper management. Remind yourself why you are at work and what you're working towards. Maintain the self-discipline to be the first one in the office and the last one out. When people ask you "what are you working so hard for?" immediately respond with "my future is waiting on me."

Pray, Meditate

Whether its prayer, meditation, or whatever it is you do during your quiet time, it's important to give yourself that time for self-analysis. Perform diagnostics on yourself. Are you becoming increasingly bothered by other events? Are some of your actions not moving you toward your purpose? Could you tweak certain actions in order to be more effective in progressing your life? Are you focusing on your purpose, or proving things to people?

If it's people you find yourself trying to prove something to or please, ask yourself why? Does that person have anything to do with fulfilling your purpose, or are they part of the mediocrity trying to hold you back?

When you're quiet and truly analyze yourself, you'll learn a lot. The Ancient Zen master Hakuin Ekaku best defined our ability to focus on ourselves when he asked, "What is the sound of one hand clapping?"

The clarity and calmness it takes to ponder an answer to such a question is the same clarity you need when focusing on yourself. When you learn yourself, you master your emotions. When you master your emotions, you become in control of your behavior. When you control your behavior, you direct your actions. When you direct your actions toward your purpose, you step closer to excellence.

Chapter 10 – Focus

Imagine you were given a rifle and had three options. First, you could close your eyes and attempt to hit the target. Second, there are several targets, and without being told which is the correct one, you must hit "the right target." The third option is to have one target, your eyes open, and you're allowed to use a scope to hone in on it.

Which do you choose? Obviously, you would choose option three. Yet, somehow in our aspirations, the majority of us either shoot blindly at our dreams, or have no idea what we're really after in the first place. How do you aim for a target that you can't identify?

Focus is the final component of excellence.

Focus is a laser-like obsession with the task at hand.

In sports, you often refer to it as an athlete being "in the zone." If you have a favorite NBA player, you probably remember their greatest performance when it seemed like they absolutely could not miss. Often times that player, in the post-game interview, says that the basket felt like it was the size of a swimming pool that they could not miss. Did the basketball hoop really change size? No. What happened? The player was focused.

When we focus all of our efforts on what we can control right now, we give ourselves the best chance for a better tomorrow.

I'm a huge fan of the Kentucky Derby, the Belmont Stakes, and the Preakness – the Triple Crown. There's just something magical about those horse races. Multi-million dollar horses all competing for the title of the fastest horse. To win, it takes the right amount of speed + endurance + strategy. The horses, who have eyes on the sides of their head for peripheral vision, often wear blinders in the race. The reason is to keep the horse focused on what's ahead and not get distracted by what's next to them, whether it be other horses or the crowd. Aside from that, the blinders ensure that the horse continues to run straight and not veer off the path set by the jockey.

Do you have blinders on in pursuit of your purpose? You should. Too many of us get caught up in the distractions of life that take our focus away from what really matters. The mediocre society of the world, which unfortunately is the vast majority, live an unfocused lifestyle, focusing on whatever grabs their attention at the moment and not their calling.

You are called to do something. Your purpose is great. You will live that purpose with intense focus.

Tough Shot

It goes without saying, it's incredibly difficult to be a sniper in the armed forces. Snipers often have to walk miles in heavy foliage to high vantage points and wait days at a time scoping out their target, waiting for the go ahead from their commander, and then taking the shot. Just getting in position and avoiding detection is a feat in itself, but that's just the beginning of the task of the sniper. The sniper must then measure factors such as wind, height, and other variables as he positions his aim for the shot. The high-powered scope on a sniper rifle can see much further than the human eye could see by itself.

In a battle that took place in November of 2009 in Afghanistan, Sniper Craig Harrison of the UK Household Calvary, redefined focus. From a distance of 1.54 miles, he locked in on to two targets, and with extreme focus and precision, set the world record for the longest shot. It was an improbable shot, further than the recommended distance for his weapon of choice, yet his focus netted him results. The sniper scope is powerful because it keeps the eye of the sniper directly on one thing, the target. The sniper isn't bothered with (and can't even see) everything else going on around him. His focus is on the target in the laser sights of the scope.

Do you have sniper-like focus? Do you zoom in on your destiny or purpose with such precision that you see nothing else but your target? The only way to truly get to where you want to go is to keep your eyes focused on two things — the end result, and the task in front of you that will get you there.

Life is a pretty simple formula that we often complicate. If you give your absolute best focused effort to each waking moment, then your "best future" will take care of itself. It's a shame that most people think merely wandering around and hoping for the best will somehow land them where they want to go. When was the last time you walked around carelessly and ended up exactly at your dream destination? It simply doesn't happen.

How'd That Happen?

When you're able to focus all of your time, energy and resources into whatever you're currently doing, with the knowledge that it's moving you toward where you want to go, you often get larger than life results, as is the case with Germany.

Germany, though small in size, is consistently in the top two exporters of goods in the entire world. It competes with countries of much larger size, such as the United States and China. How is it that a landlocked country with a fraction of the population of its much larger competitors, consistently out produce the other countries?

You might have guessed it — FOCUS. German's success is largely derived from its use of the Mittlestand

Model. The model features the work of many small to medium sized businesses, often family-owned, who each do one thing, very well. The belief is that having razor-sharp efficiency and proficiency in one area, produces greater results than being decent at a bunch of things. This enables companies that focus on a sole product or service to continually refine and sharpen their process, thus creating a better product, in a shorter amount of time, at a lesser cost. It concerns itself with long-term profit potential over current profits. Together as a country, this provides opportunities for more people and, collectively, makes Germany one of the top exporters in the world.

Do you see the parallel to your life? Are you a jack-of-all-trades who is pretty good at doing a lot of things, or are you focused on being great at something specifically? A razor cuts sharper than a butter knife. Why? Because the blade is focused. By the same token, the sharper the axe, the quicker the tree falls.

How sharp are you? Do you continually focus on sharpening strengths in your life so that they can become more efficient, or do you "get by" on natural talent?

How to Sharpen a Skill

In order to truly stay focused, you have to sharpen your skillset, especially your strengths. Much like the blade of an axe, our minds and other skills need sharpening too. Unfortunately, our skills begin to dull if not maintained, making it harder to reach our seemingly difficult purpose.

Learning Opportunities

We can sharpen a specific skill solely by paying attention to that skill and finding opportunities to learn. You could take a weekend seminar geared toward improvement, subscribe to a weekly newsletter from an expert in the field of your choice, or read more on advances and techniques that will help you improve the skill at hand. Improving your skillset creates a more efficient journey in fulfilling your purpose.

Test Yourself

Step out of your comfort zone. A blade is sharpened by being ground or tested. If it's a new language you're learning to speak, go to an area of the city where they speak it fluently and try to engage people in conversation. You'll never improve if you're not tested. If you're working on improving your communication skills to get over your fear of public speaking, speak to strangers. After that, find small community groups and get practice speaking in front of them. Remember, your pursuit of your purpose should outweigh your fear of not improving.

Teach Others

The best way to master a concept or skill is to teach it to others. Not because it makes you superior to them, but because you must truly understand a skill in order to pass it on to others. By teaching and breaking down the basics of the skill, you'll undoubtedly learn more about it yourself. Plus, the time spent teaching is time spent improving. Your focused skill will now assist you in pursuing that purpose.

How to Focus

Visualize the Target

Who would have thought that In order to discover your purpose, you would have to visualize it? It sounds so elementary, yet it's the simple philosophies that create legends. Look at your purpose, look at who you're helping, get a strong mental picture of where you're going and why. Sometimes we need to remind ourselves of why we're working so hard. Placing an extremely vivid and detailed picture in your mind of how it could be is the first step in focusing on making that dream a reality.

Create a Good Environment

As much as possible, limit your distractions. If your focus is on climbing the corporate ladder, perhaps headphones will keep other employees from distracting you and your work, or perhaps you'll have to get there early or stay late to have time to focus on getting your job done. Set yourself up in a position to be able to put your best foot forward. This means being physically and mentally prepared for each task. Though entire books could be written about it, your diet and rest play a large part in your ability to focus. Make sure you don't neglect either. In doing so, you're inhibiting your own chance at achieving excellence.

Build Momentum

The further you move toward your purpose, the more excited you will become. The closer you get to the finish line, the clearer the vision or reality becomes to you. That being said, do your best to create momentum. Small steps forward always beat a master plan or idea for "a large leap." Consistency keeps you in the moment. Staying in the moment creates momentum. Momentum brings your purpose to light and thus creates a more focused effort.

Breathe

It's a long journey, don't hold your breath. There will be times when your axe is worn down. Give yourself time to recharge and resharpen, so to speak. Take a deep breath and relax when you feel yourself getting overwhelmed. Sometimes, we have to pull over to the side of the road and remind ourselves why we're willing to continue the journey. Rest and a revisualization of what you're after will allow you to continue toward your purpose in a stronger manner.

Look Forward

The rearview mirror is small for a reason. It's to serve as a reminder of what's behind you, but not to serve as something on which to focus. The only way to truly focus is to look at what's ahead of you. That's the only thing you have the opportunity to change or direct, so it makes sense to only look in that direction. You can't hit a target that's behind you, so put all your effort into hitting the targets of today.

Your purpose is a single target, though perpetual, which is far off in the distance. Much like a sniper, with extreme focus and patience, you'll surely hit your mark.

Chapter 11 – Excellence 24/7

Excellence is being excellent, daily. It's an ideal for which to strive. To truly be a person of excellence, you must consistently possess all five qualities of excellence.

Your cheat sheet to excellence is as follows:

Purpose - Passionate pursuit of an outcome that will extend past your existence.

Drive - Unwavering advancement toward an ideal.

Habit - Consistent sequence or process that marries you to your purpose daily.

Self-Control - Actions that demonstrate the importance of the objective over the impulse.

Focus - Laser-like obsession with the task at hand.

Excellence is not a point on a map, it's a journey. It's going to take everything you have in order to fulfill your purpose.   With that being said, you have to understand that excellence doesn't come with an on/off switch. True excellence isn't categorical. It isn't limited to business or home life or whatever it may be. True excellence is synergistic; it embodies you as a person and as a result, affects all areas of your life.

Someone may be excellent in business, but terrible in relationships. That is not excellence; it's an excellent businessman. You may be excellent in your pursuit of your passion, but you don't take care of your health. You may have excellent qualities, but you aren't a person of excellence.

Strive for synergy in your life. When excellence truly becomes a part of who you are, it can't help but shine through in all areas of your life.

A table can't stand solid if it's missing a leg. A puzzle without all of the pieces isn't complete. Excellence isn't truly excellence unless you practice all five qualities of the discipline.

There's a two-step process. 1) Look at where you're going and 2) focus on giving your best to where you are at the moment.

It never fails. Solid small steps, with a solid focused direction, inevitably get you to your destination. There's a chance to practice excellence in every single aspect of your life.

It starts from the time you wake up. Excellence is in setting good habits, such as making your bed. It continues on to breakfast where self-control dictates eating a healthy meal that will fuel you through the day. Morning meditation on your purpose will provide you the visual you need throughout the day. Your actions demonstrate your drive as you maximize every minute of every hour.

Mediocrity should fear you. There is a certain look that all men and women of excellence have. Others may call it "a man on a mission." Yeah that's exactly what it is. You're on a mission and you can't and won't be stopped.

Excellence relies on momentum. Look for little things to practice excellence. Creating those habits of excellence will get you the results you're looking for.

Excellence lies in the habits of the small things. When you get your change back from the cashier, do you wad it up and throw it in your pocket? Do you think that's excellence? Instead, face each bill the correct way and put them in your wallet. It sounds silly and trivial, but it's the trivial, small things that add up.

When you get home from work, do you toss your shoes and jacket on the couch or do you hang them nicely? Again, excellence is in the small tasks. Do you respond to emails and calls promptly? Do you create a to-do list and methodically ensure you complete each task daily? Excellence is these small tasks.

We talk about synergy because excellence has a karma like or "what goes around comes around" type of effect. The more effort and focus you put into the small tasks or the things that people don't see, the more things that actually are revealed. What you do in the dark, comes to light. If you have great control in your diet, you'll see the results in your body and energy levels. If you merely talk about health and diet, but don't live a controlled life, the results will show there too.

If you routinely get to work on time and get your work done, the results speak for themselves. Aside from those results, you'll be deemed reliable. There is always a job for a reliable man.

Are you showing your partner or spouse the gratitude and care they deserve? They are a reflection of you. Your excellence toward them manifests in their appearance and mindset. If you have a significant other, look at them. Based on their appearance and happiness, are you practicing excellence with them? Do they look tired, weary, beat down and hopeless? Perhaps you should focus more on fulfilling their needs. On this journey, you are responsible for those on the ride with you, especially as a leader.

The same goes for those in the business realm. Your employees are a reflection of your leadership. You may be getting results right now, but look at the floor and see the body language of your employees. Are they overly stressed? Are they overworked? Does it look like they enjoy their job? You can work them hard and get results to appease investors, but ultimately your actions can't hide results. If you're not a benevolent boss, you'll see turnover increase. You'll start to notice work efficiency decrease, and ultimately the bottom line will fall. On the other hand, if you help the company buy into the larger purpose your business serves, give it a sense of direction and help your employees build great habits, you'll not only personally attain excellence, your company will be known as an organization of excellence too.

That's really what we're after; excellence in all we do, isn't it? Excellence in the work place, excellence in our health, excellence in our homes and relationships, and excellence in our spiritual practice. You can't have excellence without all five qualities, and you can't truly have excellence in only one area.

You're on the path to excellence right now.

Find your purpose, pursue it with passion, and get the most you can out of life. More importantly, live your life in such a manner that your performance gives the most in life to those you care about.

That's true excellence.

About The Author

Entrepreneur, Digital Strategist & Best-Selling
Author

The need to impact individuals and businesses
both online and offline is something that started many

years ago for Baylor Barbee. After a stellar high school career as a multi-sport athlete, Baylor walked-on to the Baylor University Football team and earned a full athletic scholarship.

While at Baylor University, Baylor double majored in Marketing and Entrepreneurship. Upon lettering in football and graduating, Baylor completed his Master's Degree in Education – Sports Management. Baylor served as the interim marketing director for Henry Hoops, a 501c3 non-profit geared at teaching urban youth in Waco, TX life skills as well as basketball. It was here where Baylor's passion for marketing and helping others was solidified.

Entrepreneur & Digital Strategist

Upon graduating from Baylor University, Baylor formed Silver Fox Marketing, a digital marketing firm, designed to utilize next-generation web and mobile technologies to increase customer loyalty for clients. Other solutions included product design and promotion, print and digital ad consultation and logistics management using the web. A reputation for quality work and garnering immediate results for clients provided Baylor and his team with the opportunity to manage campaigns for multi-million dollar companies, championship UFC fighters, NFL stars and other notables.

Philanthropist

Baylor co-founded a successful Hip-Hop/Rock Group with long time Baylor University teammate and friend, Trent Shelton. Sensing a need to make a positive change in their personal lives, Baylor and Trent received a higher calling to make a difference in the lives of others by way of social media and a series of online videos and live video feeds that focused on life issues and explained the role that faith often plays in the ability to cope with life's biggest challenges.

The videos and social media campaign caught on fire, catapulting Baylor and Trent to the spotlight and garnering large social media followings for both men. The aforementioned life studies, in conjunction with innovative social media strategies, created a non-profit organization that is now commonly known all over the world as RehabTime. Since its inception in 2009, RehabTime has become a global online entity inspiring millions weekly spiritually, mentally, and physically.

Best- Selling Author

Through his work with RehabTime, Baylor felt the need to connect with their thousands of followers in a way that complimented all of the community building taking place online. He, along with his partner Trent Shelton, has co-authored four books that include:

- See My Heart Not My Past

- Breaking Your Own Heart

- You're Perfect

- Know Your Circle

Sought After Speaker

Helping others identify the silver lining in life's toughest situations serves as a foundation for Baylor's speaking platform. Authenticity and a clear focus on the role excellence plays in professional development are important as well. Whether it's a small group of young business professionals or thousands at a school rally, Baylor's ability to connect and make a direct impact into the lives of attendees makes him highly sought after by schools, nonprofit organizations, churches, college athletic departments and businesses of all sizes.

Successful Athlete

Baylor resides in Dallas, Texas where he regularly competes as a Triathlete and marathoner in caused-based endurance races with the goal of bringing awareness to his many philanthropic endeavors. Always looking to make an impact, Baylor began participating in triathlons as a way to improve his own health and fitness levels, but also to inspire and encourage others to set their goals high and believe anything is possible.

Baylor on the Web

http://www.BaylorBarbee.com

http://www.facebook.com/BaylorBarbeeWin

http://www.twitter.com/BaylorBarbee

Other Books by the Author

(Co-author – Trent Shelton)

Breaking Your Own Heart

How many times have you cried tears into your pillowcase with a broken heart shouting, "WHY DID I LET THIS HAPPEN AGAIN?!" We've all been there, shed those tears and felt that heartache.

You're tired of having your heart broken, aren't you? You're tired of the nonsense, right? The hardest concept to grasp in dealing with broken hearts is this simple fact:

You break your own heart.

Only you know your heart. Let this e-manual guide you toward understanding how you break your own heart and more importantly, how to avoid breaking it.

See My Heart Not My Past

All of us have made mistakes we would like to forget and most of us may not be content with where we are, but we do wish to see a better tomorrow.

Join us on this figurative thirty day journey focused on leaving your past behind you and becoming the individual you always wanted to be.

Change starts with you.

Change starts now.

You're Perfect

Are you tired of feeling insignificant? Are you tired of feeling like you'll never find "the one" for you?

Don't you know you're Perfect?!

"You're Perfect" aims to increase your self-worth by helping you understand that God made you Perfect for the heart that's meant to love you. In "You're Perfect," you'll not only learn about the great qualities of yourself, you'll learn what True Love is and what it's not. More importantly you'll learn how to apply those principles to help you find the Heart that's meant to Love You.

Know Your Circle

Your Circle has the power to make you or break you. You are the company you keep and that company will ultimately help lead you to your dreams or your destruction.

Know Your Circle will not only help you identify the bad apples in your circle, it will help you build an unbreakable team.